Publishers Accepting Children's Picture Books

Published by Gecko Tales Publishing

https://geckotales.com.au/

For most authors of Picture Books, the initial aim is to hold the book in your hand or to share it with family, friends or perhaps the rest of the world. To do this, it needs to get **published**!

The benchmark of success in most author's eyes is to be published by a traditional publishing house Like Scholastic, Penguin Random House, Hachette, Allen & Unwin, or Pan Macmillan, and while being published by one of them would be the Holy Grail, there are many wonderful publishing houses available to the budding writer and/or illustrator.

I have researched and compiled a list of publishers accepting unsolicited picture book submissions.

These lists often change as publishers close to unsolicited submissions, or are only open for a short period. So you will still need to do your research on each to determine those accepting picture books and ones that publish similar to your style.

Australian Publishers Accepting Picture Books

Affirm Press

HTTP://AFFIRMPRESS.COM.AU/SUBMISSIONS/

PICTURE BOOK SUBMISSIONS ONLY ACCEPTED FIRST MONDAY OF THE MONTH

An independent Melbourne-based publisher dedicated to publishing great Australian stories, big ideas, and the most engaging local and international authors.

Big Sky Publishing

HTTPS://BIGSKYPUBLISHING.COM.AU/ABOUT-US/SUBMITTING-A-MANUSCRIPT/

An independent Australian publisher proudly focusing on supporting Australian authors, illustrators and content

Bloomsbury Spark

HTTPS://WWW.BLOOMSBURY.COM/AU/CHILDRENS/

Shortlisted for Children's Publisher of the Year 2018 for both the Independent Publishing Group Award and the British Book Awards.

DoctorZed

HTTPS://DOCTORZED.COM/SUBMISSIONS/

With over 200+ titles from over 100+ international authors, our wide range of titles have **one common aim**—to deliver Goodness, Truth and Beauty. Our titles take the form of inspiring stories, triumph of good over evil and are heartfelt and purpose driven.

EK Books

HTTP://EKBOOKS.ORG/SUBMISSIONS

EK is a publisher of children's picture books only. Our motto is 'books with heart on issues that matter' and our books are aimed primarily at children aged 4 to 8.

Empowering Resources

HTTP://WWW.EMPOWERINGRESOURCES.COM.AU/NEW-SUBMISSIONS/

Looking for manuscripts that are nurturing, educational and empowering. We love reading stories that encourage meaningful conversations through a strong narrative, with relatable characters and an organic message.

ETHICOOL BOOKS
HTTPS://ETHICOOLBOOKS.COM
Looking for remarkable children's books about the world's big issues, inspiring kids to create positive change.

FORD STREET
HTTPS://FORDSTREETPUBLISHING.COM/
We publish around fifteen titles a year, ranging from picture books through to novels for older readers. Ford Street's publisher is renowned Australian author, Paul Collins, who has written extensively for both the local and international markets.

HARDIE GRANT EGMONT
HTTPS://HARDIEGRANT.COM/AU/HARDIE-GRANT-CHILDRENS-PUBLISHING/
Hardie Grant Children's Publishing is the children's division of the largest independent publisher in Australia, and the home of innovative, inclusive and entertaining books from tots to teens.

HINKLER BOOKS

HTTPS://WWW.HINKLER.COM.AU

Hinkler is a global, independent publisher based in Melbourne, Australia. Our mission is to surprise and delight every child, adult and retailer we meet by publishing books with a difference. For booklovers of all ages we have a quality book, kit, game or puzzle for you.

IP KIDZ

HTTPS://IPOZ.BIZ/IP-KIDZ/

WE'RE OPEN FROM MARCH – DECEMBER

We are the second largest publisher of literary titles in Queensland. A hybrid publisher, we offer royalty contracts to high-quality work, but also use our expertise to assist corporate clients and individuals who want to publish material in print and/or digital form.

LAKE PRESS

HTTPS://LAKEPRESS.COM.AU/

Lake Press is an independent book publisher, specialising in illustrated books primarily for children.

LARRIKIN HOUSE

HTTPS://LARRIKINHOUSE.COM/SUBMISSIONS

We're passionately committed to creating quirky, original & humorous kid-focussed books. Over 70% of our books so far are from first-time published authors & illustrators!

NEW FRONTIER

HTTPS://WWW.NEWFRONTIER.COM.AU/

New Frontier was established in Australia in 2002 with the motto 'to inspire, educate and uplift children'. Our expertise is in primary school age books.

NEW HOLLAND PUBLISHERS

HTTP://AU.NEWHOLLANDPUBLISHERS.COM/SUBMISSIONS

With offices in Sydney and Auckland, New Holland drives books into fresh new channels and explores all avenues to maximise sales and act in the best interests of their authors.

ODYSSEY BOOKS

HTTP://ODYSSEYBOOKS.COM.AU/SUBMISSIONS/

We invest in epic journeys, adventurous voyages, and intellectual or spiritual quests. Readers are sure to find a book within our range of titles to challenge, inspire and entertain.

PADEMELON PRESS

HTTPS://PADEMELONPRESS.COM.AU/

The mission of Pademelon Press is to publish and distribute quality Australian early childhood teacher resource and reference books to assist teachers and carers in their task of educating and caring for children.

WOMBAT BOOKS

HTTPS://WOMBATBOOKS.COM.AU/

Wombat Books has been sharing stories and creating memories with families for over ten years. As an independent boutique publisher, we love to find those unique stories that connect us all with readable and loveable characters.

Red Paper Kite

HTTPS://WWW.REDPAPERKITE.COM/REDPAPERKITE
RED paper kite's focus is on children's picture books.

Starfish Bay

HTTP://STARFISHBAYPUBLISHING.COM.AU/
Starfish Bay Publishing is an independent publishing house located in Adelaide, Australia. We are dedicated to publishing quality picture books for children primarily aged between 3 to 8.

Walker Books

HTTPS://WWW.WALKERBOOKS.COM.AU/
Walker Books Australia has been bringing the best of children's publishing to Australian children for over 20 years and is recognised as a market leader in quality children's books.

WILD ORANGE

HTTPS://WILDORANGEPUBLISHING.COM/

Wild Orange Publishing is a small press publishing company that produces exceptional and unforgettable children's books

USBORNE

HTTPS://USBORNE.COM/AU/

Usborne is one of the world's leading independent children's book publishers and proud to be a family business.

YELLOW BRICK BOOKS

HTTPS://WWW.YELLOWBRICKBOOKS.COM.AU/

In picture books, we are looking for stories that are clever, different, or out of the ordinary. We're also hunting for new illustrators for current and future projects.

Other Publishers Accepting Picture Books

Holiday House

HTTPS://HOLIDAYHOUSE.COM

An American publishing house founded with the purpose of publishing only children's books. Holiday House publishes the award-winning I Like to Read® series of picture books for emergent readers

Arbordale Publishing

HTTPS://ARBORDALEPUBLISHING.COM

Arbordale books spark excitement for reading with engaging stories and a nonfiction "For Creative Minds" activity section. Kids can explore the "how" and "why" of science topics!

Immedium

HTTPS://IMMEDIUM.COM

Immedium publishes engaging characters and entertaining stories that scratch the surface of possibility.

LEE & LOW BOOKS
HTTPS://LEEANDLOW.COM
Passionate about publishing beautiful and authentic diverse books for young readers

ALBERT WHITMAN & COMPANY
HTTPS://ALBERTWHITMAN.COM
When Albert Whitman was founded more than a century ago, our goal was simple: make good books that kids want to read. Today, we continue this tradition, guided by a deeper mission to create stories that also educate and empower children.

CHARLESBRIDGE PUBLISHING
HTTPS://CHARLESBRIDGE.COM
Charlesbridge publishes high-quality books for children, with a goal of creating lifelong readers and lifelong learners. Our books encourage reading and discovery in the classroom, library, and home.

Free Spirit Publishing
HTTPS://FREESPIRIT.COM
Free Spirit provides children and teens—and the adults who care for and about them—with the tools they need to think for themselves, overcome challenges, and make a difference in the world.

Little Tiger Press
HTTPS://LITTLETIGER.CO.UK
The **Little Tiger Group** was founded in 1987 by The Bhatia Family. We started life as a publisher of picture books and grew organically, gradually exploring different formats and genres, always innovating and focused on producing beautiful, engaging books for children and young people.

Workman Publishing
HTTPS://WORKMAN.COM
Located in the heart of New York's Greenwich Village, in a converted printers' building, our offices are high-energy and creative, filled with people who are passionate about what they do.

Kane Miller

HTTP://WWW.FRIENDS.KANEMILLER.COM/

Kane Miller Books specializes in award-winning children's books from around the world. Our books bring the children of the world closer to each other, sharing stories and ideas, while exploring cultural differences and similarities.

Tilbury House Publishers

HTTPS://TILBURYHOUSE.COM

Our children's book division became a major emphasis beginning in the early 1990s, and since then we have continued to publish award-winning children's picture books for both the trade and education markets

Abdo Publishing

HTTPS://ABDOBOOKS.COM/

For over 30 years, ABDO has been publishing exceptional children's PreK–12 educational titles for libraries and schools.

ABRAMS BOOK

HTTPS://ABRAMSBOOKS.COM

Founded in 1949, ABRAMS was the first company in the United States to specialize in publishing art and illustrated books, ranging from middle grade to young adult fiction to picture books to board books

ALLEN AND UNWIN

HTTPS://ALLENANDUNWIN.COM

Allen & Unwin is Australia's leading independent publisher and is the 2020 Publisher of the Year. We have been voted "Publisher of the Year" fourteen times including in the inaugural award in 1992 and eleven times since 2000.

ANNICK PRESS

HTTPS://ANNICKPRESS.COM

Annick Press is a proudly independent children's publisher based in Toronto, Canada. Annick is recognized as one of the most innovative publishers of fiction and nonfiction for children and young adults.

ANDERSEN PRESS

HTTPS://ANDERSENPRESS.CO.UK

Andersen Press, founded in 1976, publishes some of the most well-known and best loved names in the world of children's books.

ANDREWS MCMEEL

HTTPS://ANDREWSMCMEEL.COM

We're passionate about publishing authors with a distinct point of view. We offer an individualized, flexible approach to publishing success by respecting the author's vision as the primary source of inspiration at every stage of the editorial, marketing and distribution process.

BAREFOOT BOOKS

HTTPS://BAREFOOTBOOKS.COM

Creating visually captivating books that celebrate diversity, spark curiosity and capture children's imaginations.

BLOOMSBURY

HTTPS://WWW.BLOOMSBURY.COM/US/

Established in 1998 and located in midtown Manhattan, Bloomsbury USA is a general interest publisher of adult and children's books which has become known for both its high quality fiction and non-fiction for adults and children as well as its extensive Academic publishing from the world's most recognized experts.

BLUE APPLE BOOKS

HTTPS://BLUEAPPLEBOOKS.COM

Blue Apple Books has published hundreds of children's books since we began the company in 2003.

BOXER BOOKS

HTTP://WWW.BOXERBOOKSLTD.CO.UK/

Our focus is publishing new and established international authors and illustrators, working with them to develop their personal style and create books that children and adults can enjoy together.

BUSTER BOOKS

HTTPS://BUSTERBOOKS.CO.UK

As an independent publisher, we depend on the passion and creativity of our employees, illustrators and authors.

CHRONICLE BOOKS

HTTPS://WWW.CHRONICLEBOOKS.COM/

Inspired by the enduring magic and importance of books. We create exceptional publishing that's instantly recognizable for its spirit, creativity, and value.

CHICKEN HOUSE

HTTPS://CHICKENHOUSEBOOKS.COM

Chicken House is a small, highly individual children's book publishing company with an enthusiasm for new fiction. Chicken House books have found huge popularity with children, parents, teachers and librarians around the world.

Epigram Books

HTTPS://EPIGRAMBOOKS.SG

Epigram Books has published all manner of fiction and non-fiction, from novels to picture books, memoirs to cookbooks, graphic novels to poetry.

Floris Books

HTTPS://FLORISBOOKS.CO.UK

The largest children's book publisher in Scotland. We publish board and picture books for 0-7 year olds, including international stories in translation and nostalgic classics.

Flying Eye Books

HTTPS://FLYINGEYEBOOKS.COM

Flying Eye Books (FEB, for short) is the children's imprint of award-winning visual publishing house Nobrow. Established in early 2013, FEB sought to retain the same attention to detail in design and excellence in illustrated content as its parent publisher, but with a focus on the craft of children's storytelling and non-fiction.

Goelette International

HTTPS://GOELETTEINTERNATIONAL.COM

the leader in puzzle series throughout French Canada, developing a catalogue with a very specific purpose: provide diversified, affordable and high-quality books for all ages.

Hachette US

HTTPS://HACHETTEBOOKGROUP.COM

Hachette Book Group (HBG) publishes children's books across all genres and reading levels. From picture books for toddlers to colorful and engaging graphic novels for kids, we offer timeless and treasured works for all ages.

Harpercollins

HTTPS://HARPERCOLLINS.CO.UK

Inspire a lifelong love of reading with our award-winning children's books, timeless classics and brilliantly funny blockbusters. HarperCollins Children's Books is home to some of the most popular authors in children's literature today.

HOUGHTON MIFFLIN HARCOURT

HTTPS://WWW.HMHCO.COM/

We help you inspire a new generation of leaders, thinkers, and doers

HOGS BACK BOOKS

HTTP://WWW.HOGSBACKBOOKS.COM/

We publish picture books for readers aged up to 10 years. Our aim is to produce quality books for children to enjoy and treasure by matching great stories with fresh and original illustrations.

LION HUDSON

HTTPS://LIONHUDSON.COM

At Lion Hudson, a Part of the SPCK Group, we publish books and other media for children and adults to help you grow in your Christian faith.

LITTLE TIGER
HTTPS://LITTLETIGER.CO.UK

The Little Tiger Group was founded in 1987 by The Bhatia Family. We started life as a publisher of picture books and grew organically, gradually exploring different formats and genres, always innovating and focused on producing beautiful, engaging books for children and young people.

MAGINATION PRESS
HTTPS://WWW.APA.ORG/PUBS/MAGINATION

Magination Press is the children's book imprint of the American Psychological Association. Through our publishing we share with the world mental health expertise and psychological knowledge.

MIGHTY MEDIA PRESS
HTTPS://MIGHTYMEDIAPRESS.COM/

Delivering captivating books and media that ignite a child's curiosity, imagination, social awareness, and sense of adventure.

NOSY CROW

HTTPS://NOSYCROW.COM

Nosy Crow is a multi-award-winning, independent children's publishing company. We make child-focused, parent-friendly children's books for ages 0-12.

PRIDDY BOOKS

HTTPS://WWW.PRIDDYBOOKS.COM/

At Priddy Books, we publish innovative titles for babies, toddlers and young children.

PETER PAUPER PRESS

HTTPS://WWW.PETERPAUPER.COM/

Bring a sense of exploration, new ideas, and imaginings to little ones with our original children's picture books—all while sharing quality "together" time with your loved ones. Peter Pauper Press is proud to publish uniquely talented picture book authors and illustrators who are bringing their enchantments to life.

Random House

HTTPS://WWW.PENGUIN.CO.UK/GENRES/CHILDREN.HTML

By bringing together the greatest stories, brands and authors of any global children's publisher, Penguin Random House Children's are here to help create and rediscover heroes for each new generation.

Really Decent Books

HTTPS://WWW.REALLYDECENTBOOKS.CO.UK/

Really Decent Books is a small, independent children's publishing company, based in the beautiful city of Bath. We publish high-quality baby, toddler and pre-school books for children aged from 0 to 7 with well-known illustrators and new talent.

Sterling Publishing

HTTPS://WWW.STERLINGPUBLISHING.COM/

Is an Innovative and forward-thinking publishing company committed to creating books that educate, inspire and entertain.

BONNIER BOOKS

HTTPS://WWW.BONNIERBOOKS.CO.UK/

Bonnier Books UK is home to 14 adult and children's imprints, publishing across a wide variety of genres for different ages.

IMAGINE THAT PUBLISHING

HTTPS://WWW.IMAGINETHAT.COM/

Independent publisher and packager that have been creating books that inspire children to read, learn, play and create for over twenty years.

TUTTLE PUBLISHING

HTTPS://WWW.TUTTLEPUBLISHING.COM/

Our core values remain as strong today as they were then—to publish best-in-class books which bring people together one page at a time.

QED Publishing

HTTPS://WWW.QUARTOKNOWS.COM/QED-PUBLISHING

Working with acclaimed authors and consultants, QED Publishing is going from strength to strength. Its mission is simple – to create fresh, informative, high-quality books that will appeal to children, parents and teachers alike.

Usborne

HTTPS://USBORNE.COM/AU/

Usborne is one of the world's leading independent children's book publishers and proud to be a family business.

Walker

HTTPS://WWW.WALKER.CO.UK/

The Walker Books Group is one of the world's leading independent publishers of books and content for children. This vibrant international group includes Walker Books UK, London; Candlewick Press, Somerville, Massachusetts; and Walker Books Australia, based in Sydney and Auckland

WORKMAN

HTTPS://WWW.WORKMAN.COM/

Workman Publishing Co., Inc., is an independently owned family of publishers, including Workman Publishing, Algonquin Books of Chapel Hill, Algonquin Young Readers, Artisan, Storey Publishing, and Timber Press. We are also partners with The Experiment, duopress, Erewhon Books, and Familius.

I COMPILED THIS LIST PRIMARILY FOR PICTURE BOOK AUTHORS, HOWEVER; IT IS EQUALLY RELEVANT TO ALL GENRES OF CHILDREN'S BOOK WRITING.

OK SO THAT'S IT FOR NOW.

ALL THE BEST WITH YOUR CHILDREN'S BOOK WRITING CAREER.

THE KIDSLIT GUY

ARE YOU LOOKING FOR HELP TO WRITE THAT AMAZING CHILDREN'S PICTURE BOOK?

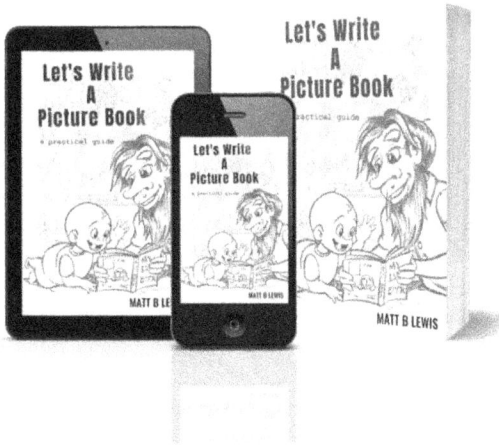

WELL, THIS BOOK LETS YOU DO JUST THAT! WRITTEN WITH A PRACTICAL APPROACH TO EVERY FACET OF THE PICTURE BOOK MARKET, YOU CAN OVERCOME THAT SELF-DOUBT AND BANISH THE DREADED BLANK PAGE FOREVER. WITH HIS PHILOSOPHY OF K.I.D.S KEEPING IT DELIGHTFULLY SIMPLE, MATT B PRESENTS CURRENT PROCESSES, PRACTICAL EXERCISES AND A WEALTH OF INDUSTRY INFORMATION.

HTTP://MYBOOK.TO/LETSWRITEAPICTUREBOOK

LET'S WRITE A PICTURE BOOK

OTHER BOOKS FOR KIDSLIT AUTHORS

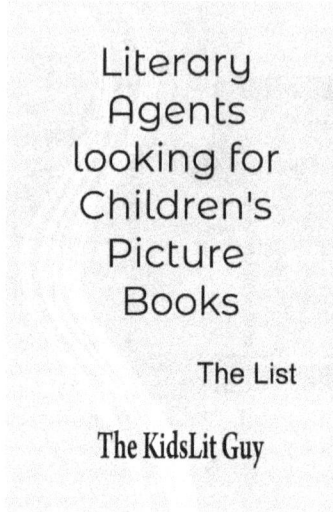

Literary
Agents
looking for
Children's
Picture
Books

The List

The KidsLit Guy

http://mybook.to/LitAgentPictureBooks

www.ingramcontent.com/pod-product-compliance
Lightning Source LLC
Chambersburg PA
CBHW021123020426
42331CB00004B/605